Life Lessons from the Book of Ruth

Susan D. Elliott

Published by Atreju Gold, 2023.

Also by Susan D. Elliott

Let Your Light Shine
Life Lessons from the Book of Ruth
The 7 Churches of Asia

Table of Contents

Thank you for encouraging me to write. I love you to
the moon and back!

"Blessed be the LORD, which hath not left thee this day without a kinsman."— Ruth 4:14

A Note to the Reader

This study was originally presented at a Ladies' Day event at the Star City church of Christ in Roanoke, Virginia. It was prepared with the goal of encouraging women to grow in faith, deepen their understanding of Scripture, and apply God's Word to everyday life.

It is my prayer that the lessons found here will be useful for personal study, Bible classes, and group discussion, and that they will encourage you to walk faithfully with God in every season of life.

How to Use This Study

This book is designed for both individual and group Bible study. Each lesson includes Scripture-based teaching, discussion questions, and reflection prompts to help deepen understanding and encourage spiritual growth.

For individual study, take time to read the Scripture passages carefully, reflect on the questions provided, and consider how the lessons apply to your own life.

For group or class use, the discussion questions may be used to encourage participation and thoughtful conversation. Leaders may choose to focus on selected questions based on time and group needs.

Whether studied alone or with others, it is my hope that this study will help strengthen your faith and draw you closer to God.

Historical Background

THE BOOK OF RUTH IS unique among the books of the Bible. Only two books in Scripture are titled with the name of a woman: Esther and Ruth. According to an article titled "The Book of Ruth Introduction," only two books in the Bible are associated with non-Jews. One is the Gospel account of Luke, and the other is the book of Ruth.

Interestingly, Ruth tells the story of a Moabite woman who chose to follow God during the period of the Judges. She became the daughter-in-law of Rahab the harlot through her marriage to Boaz. Although no author is identified within the text, many historians believe the book of Ruth was written by Samuel.

Matthew 1:5 records that Rahab and Salmon had a son named Boaz, who later married Ruth. Their son, Obed, became the grandfather of King David. Because Ruth was the daughter-in-law of Rahab, many believe the events of the book of Ruth occurred early in the period of the Judges. Rahab, the harlot, famously hid the spies in Jericho, as recorded in Joshua 2. Because of her faith, her family was spared when Jericho fell.

Many scholars speculate about the purpose of the book of Ruth. Some suggest that David's Moabite heritage was questioned during his reign. These scholars believe the book was written to demonstrate that his Moabite lineage came from an honorable woman who faithfully followed God. Ruth is often compared to the virtuous woman described in Proverbs 31:10–31.

The book of Ruth illustrates familial love, marriage, and the providence of God. Most importantly, it shows that God accepts those who follow Him. Boaz serves as a representation of Christ. He is referred to several times as the "kinsman-redeemer," and in this role, he redeems Ruth according to Judaic law. Ruth, a Gentile, is joined to Boaz through marriage, just as we are joined to Christ through the church, the bride of Christ. Though the book of Ruth contains only four chapters, it offers powerful lessons through her example.

Chapter One: Ruth Stood Strong in Adversity

Where thou diest, will I die, and there will I be buried: the LORD do so to me, and more also, if ought but death part thee and me. When she saw that she was steadfastly minded to go with her, then she left speaking unto her.
Ruth 1:17–18

THE BOOK OF RUTH BEGINS during a great famine in the land of Israel. The famine was so severe that a man named Elimelech, from the tribe of Judah, left Bethlehem and traveled to the land of Moab with his wife and their two sons. Scripture does not indicate the ages of Elimelech or his sons, but they lived in Moab for some time. While there, Elimelech died, leaving his wife Naomi alone with their two sons, Mahlon and Chilion (Ruth 1:1–3).

While living in Moab, the sons married outside of Israel, taking Moabite women as wives (v. 4). One was named Orpah, and the other Ruth. These women entered into marriage with men who followed Jehovah God. Later verses in the first chapter of Ruth indicate that neither Ruth nor Orpah had converted or fully committed themselves to following God at that point, despite marrying into a Jewish family.

According to Judd H. Burton, author of the article "Chemosh: Lord of the Moabites," the Moabites were known for worshipping the god Chemosh, whose name may mean "destroyer," "subduer," or "fish god." The Bible records in II Kings 11:7 that Solomon built a high place for Chemosh on the mountain east of Jerusalem. That high place was later destroyed by King Josiah, as recorded in II Kings 23:13. Chemosh was not worshipped solely through animal sacrifice but also through human sacrifice. II Kings 3:27a states, "Then he [the king of Moab] took his eldest son that should have reigned in his stead and offered him for a burnt offering upon the wall."

Chemosh—not Jehovah—was the god of the people of Moab. It was in this land that Naomi found herself without her husband and her sons. It was there that she heard the Lord had prospered the land of Israel (v. 6), and it was there that she determined it was time to return home. Like the son who squandered his inheritance in the parable of the prodigal son (Luke 15:11–32), Naomi knew that Bethlehem was where she needed to go.

How many of us live our lives surrounded by the evils of society? How many of us feel battered or beaten down by the circumstances in which we find ourselves? We must remember that even in our weakest moments, we can find the strength to remain faithful and follow God. We are daughters of the King—baptized believers who have taken an oath, so to speak, to follow God no matter what comes our way.

There will be times when we find ourselves in inhospitable environments. We may even face our own personal horror stories, but we can overcome them if we turn to God our Father. We must hold fast to our faith (Hebrews 10:19–25) and reach out to Him through prayer (Matthew 7:7–11), trusting that God answers our prayers. We should never doubt it. All of us have endured circumstances that felt unbearable at the time, yet we leaned on God for strength and found that we could overcome them in His arms.

Several years ago, I went out to eat with a group of ladies from our student wives' class at the Memphis School of Preaching. I was young, unmarried, and a junior in high school. That evening, we chose to eat at a Shoney's in Memphis near Knight Arnold. If you've ever been to Memphis, you know that area can be rough. I was sitting with my back to the door and the cash register. A friend sat beside me, and my mother sat across from me. We were enjoying ourselves when, in an instant, screaming erupted and what sounded like gunfire pierced the air. Our happiness immediately turned into unadulterated fear.

I grew up in a small town in Central Texas, about forty-five minutes from Killeen, where Fort Hood is located. During my first year of high school, a man from Belton, Texas, drove his pickup truck into a Luby's cafeteria in Killeen and opened fire, killing twenty-four people before taking his own life. A few months later, another tragedy occurred in Austin, where four teenage girls were murdered at a I Can't Believe It's Yogurt! shop. Austin is also about forty-five minutes from my hometown.

As we crouched beneath the tables at Shoney's, these tragedies were vivid in our minds. We were terrified, and we prayed. Eventually, we were escorted to the back of the restaurant and brought to safety. We later learned that what we thought were gunshots were actually the sound of the safety glass door shattering as the robber struck it while fleeing. Some of the ladies in our group had been standing at the register when the robbery occurred. One was even pushed to the floor. Yet in that moment of terror, we clung to God and found peace in knowing that if we lost our lives, we had a home with Him.

We all experience tragedy. We have all known fear and grief. What defines us is how we respond during those moments. In our darkest times, we must remember that God is our strength and refuge, a very present help in trouble (Psalm 46:1).

Naomi certainly knew pain and loss. She had lost three of the most important people in her life. Yet, even in the depths of despair, she found comfort through God and strength through a woman who was not her flesh and blood but was just as dear to her.

Notice Ruth 1:16–17:

"And Ruth said, Intreat me not to leave thee, or to return from following after thee: for whither thou goest, I will go; and where thou lodgest, I will lodge: thy people shall be my people, and thy God my God: Where thou diest, will I die, and there will I be buried: the LORD do so to me, and more also, if ought but death part thee and me."

These verses reveal much about Ruth's character. Ruth had also lost her husband, and although she still had family in Moab (Ruth 1:8), she chose to remain with her mother-in-law. She followed Naomi to Bethlehem and made the decision to put away Chemosh and follow Jehovah.

Ruth loved her family—not only her biological family. How many of us would leave our homeland to follow our mothers-in-law to a foreign land with unfamiliar customs? Some of us might be willing. Others have already made similar choices and know how difficult they can be. Yet many would likely remain behind, as Ruth's sister-in-law Orpah did.

Ruth was courageous and deeply empathetic to Naomi's loss. She understood the pain of losing a husband and longed to stay with Naomi because she recognized her suffering and wanted to give her strength.

One of the most beautiful outcomes of hardship is the ability to help others. As women, we can often relate to those facing similar trials. As a preacher's wife, my husband and I have served in some difficult congregations. We have known the pain of rejection and the feeling of being outsiders. While those experiences were painful at the time, they taught me valuable lessons that I can now share with younger preacher's wives. Through trial, I learned to be myself and to strive to please God rather than man. Ultimately, God is the One who matters. Through these experiences, I came to truly understand Philippians 4:13: "I can do all things through Christ which strengtheneth me." And you can too.

Some of us have lost children. Others have children who have fallen into sin. Some struggle with addiction or endure loveless marriages. Some may not know where their next meal will come from.

You know at least one sister who has faced these trials. That sister may be you. If so, remember that God carried you through those moments. Share your story. Help a sister in need. Be a Ruth to your family and friends.

There is an acronym often shared online: FROG—Fully Rely On God. Sisters, we must.

These questions are intended to encourage discussion and further study of Ruth's faithfulness and perseverance during times of hardship. Whether studied individually or in a group setting, they are designed to help you reflect on how trusting God through adversity can strengthen both your faith and your ability to support others.

- Why did Elimelech move his family into the land of Moab?
- What were the names of Elimelech and Naomi's sons?
- What were the names of Elimelech and Naomi's daughters-in-law?
- Who went with Naomi back to Jerusalem?
- How do we know we can overcome? Provide supporting Bible verses.
- What do we learn about Ruth's character from Ruth 1:16–17?
- We all go through pain. What benefit can our struggles be to others?
- What can you do to help those around you who have experienced similar circumstances?
- Discuss Philippians 4:13. How does this verse apply to your life?
- What has helped keep you faithful to God during times of struggle?

Refining Your Thoughts

Take a moment to reflect on what you've studied. How can you apply what you've learned? What is one thing you can do today to become a better you? Whether you are studying individually or as a class, think of specific ways to practice these lessons in your everyday life—and commit to them. Together, we can grow as Christian women and become the kind of women God wants us to be.

Chapter Two: Ruth Had a Mind to Work

*A**nd she said, I pray you, let me glean and gather after the reapers among the sheaves: so she came, and hath continued even from the morning until now, that she tarried a little in the house.*

Ruth 2:7

THE SECOND CHAPTER of Ruth paints a clear portrait of a hard-working woman. Verse two records a conversation between Ruth and Naomi: "And Ruth the Moabitess said unto Naomi, Let me now go to the field, and glean ears of corn after him in whose sight I shall find grace. And she said unto her, Go, my daughter." Ruth desired to work, to carry her weight, and to help provide for herself and her mother-in-law. Her desire led to action, and in verse three we see her gleaning—picking up the leftover grain after the harvest—in the fields behind the reapers. She gathered what fell to the ground, the remnants left behind.

Most of us have never harvested a large crop by hand and know only from stories how demanding that kind of labor can be. My mother-in-law grew up in South Texas, where her parents raised thirteen children in a two-bedroom house. Every member of the family worked in the fields, picking cotton to earn extra income. It was exhausting, back-breaking work.

Ruth did not shy away from what needed to be done to feed herself and Naomi. Jerusalem experiences two primary seasons—summer and winter. Harvest time typically falls during the spring months, when temperatures range from 86°F to 104°F. The heat increases steadily throughout the day before cooling rapidly in the evening.

Ruth would have begun her workday in the cool of the morning and continued as the temperature climbed higher and higher. Jerusalem is known for its bright, cloudless skies. Imagine laboring for hours in an open field with no shade from passing clouds, or being caught in sudden dust storms that bring dry winds and intense heat. Yet Ruth worked willingly—and she worked happily.

Her diligence did not go unnoticed.

Notice verses 4–9:

And, behold, Boaz came from Bethlehem, and said unto the reapers, The Lord be with you. And they answered him, The Lord bless thee. Then said Boaz unto his servant that was set over the reapers, Whose damsel is this? And the servant that was set over the reapers answered and said, It is the Moabitish damsel that came back with Naomi out of the country of Moab: And she said, I pray you, let me glean and gather after the reapers among the sheaves: so she came, and hath continued even from the morning until now, that she tarried a little in the house. Then said Boaz unto Ruth, Hearest thou not, my daughter? Go not to glean in another field, neither go from hence, but abide here fast by my maidens: Let thine eyes be on the field that they do reap,

and go thou after them: have I not charged the young men that they shall not touch thee? And when thou art athirst, go unto the vessels, and drink of that which the young men have drawn.

Boaz noticed Ruth immediately and inquired about her. He spoke to her, promised to provide for her needs—such as water—ensured her safety, and instructed her to glean only in his fields.

Isn't it interesting how God uses people who are willing to work? Consider the apostles Christ chose to follow Him. He selected men who understood labor and responsibility. Several apostles were fishermen, one was a tax collector, and the Apostle Paul supported himself as a tentmaker (Mark 1:16, 22; Matthew 4:18–22; Matthew 9:9; Acts 18:3).

Christ placed great importance on workers. Why do you think this is? The Christian life is not easy and often requires sacrifice. This was true for first-century Christians and remains true today. The Apostle Paul writes, "Therefore, my beloved brethren, be ye steadfast, unmovable, always abounding in the work of the Lord, forasmuch as ye know that your labor is not in vain in the Lord" (I Corinthians 15:58).

When Christ chose His apostles, He knew His earthly ministry would be brief—only about three years. He knew the kingdom would need faithful workers once He was gone. Matthew 28:19–20 records His command: "Go ye therefore, and teach all nations, baptizing them in the name of the Father, and of the Son, and of the Holy Ghost: Teaching them to observe all things whatsoever I have commanded you: and, lo, I am with you always, even unto the end of the world." Christ gave the apostles a responsibility and expected them to fulfill it. He expects the same of us today.

Though Ruth lived during the period of the Judges and likely had no knowledge of God's plan to bring a Messiah into the world, she became an essential part of that plan. Her devotion to Naomi and her willingness to work drew the attention of Boaz—and ultimately placed her within God's greater purpose

These questions are designed to encourage discussion and further study of Ruth's willingness to work and her faithful attitude in daily responsibilities. As you reflect—individually or in a group—consider how diligence, humility, and a strong work ethic can be expressions of faith and service to God in your own life.

- What did Ruth ask Naomi at the beginning of chapter two?
- What does it mean to glean?
- What kind of work is gleaning?
- How many seasons does Jerusalem have?
- What were the weather conditions under which Ruth worked?
- What kind of people did Christ choose to be His apostles?
- What were the apostles' professional backgrounds?
- Christians in the first century were expected to be hard workers. Is that expectation still true today? Why or why not?
- What Bible verses teach that Christians have a responsibility to work, and what is that work?
- What qualities in Ruth attracted the attention she received from Boaz?

Refining Your Thoughts

Take a moment to reflect on what you've studied. How can you apply what you've learned? What is one thing you can do today to become a better you? Whether you are studying individually or as a class, think of practical ways to apply the lessons from this chapter in your everyday life—and commit to them. Together, we can grow as Christian women and become the kind of women God wants us to be.

Chapter Three: Ruth Had a Good Name

"*A good name is rather to be chosen than great riches, and loving favour rather than silver and gold.*" Proverbs 22:1

RUTH 2:11 RECORDS BOAZ'S words to Ruth: "And Boaz answered and said unto her, It hath fully been shewed me, all that thou hast done unto thy mother-in-law since the death of thine husband: and how thou hast left thy father and thy mother, and the land of thy nativity, and art come unto a people which thou knewest not heretofore." Later, Boaz declares in Ruth 3:11 that "all the city" knew Ruth was a virtuous woman. Ruth was a woman of great character, and those around her recognized it. What a wonderful compliment it is to be known as a virtuous woman.

There are many similarities between Ruth and the virtuous woman described in Proverbs 31:10–31. Hopefully, we can strive to reflect those same qualities in our own lives. Take a moment to consider the virtuous woman described in Scripture.

The passage states:

Who can find a virtuous woman? For her price is far above rubies. The heart of her husband doth safely trust in

her, so that he shall have no need of spoil. She will do him good and not evil all the days of her life. She seeketh wool, and flax, and worketh willingly with her hands.

She is like the merchants' ships; she bringeth her food from afar. She riseth also while it is yet night, and giveth meat to her household, and a portion to her maidens. She considereth a field, and buyeth it: with the fruit of her hands she planteth a vineyard. She girdeth her loins with strength, and strengtheneth her arms. She perceiveth that her merchandise is good: her candle goeth not out by night. She layeth her hands to the spindle, and her hands hold the distaff.

She stretcheth out her hand to the poor; yea, she reacheth forth her hands to the needy. She is not afraid of the snow for her household: for all her household are clothed with scarlet. She maketh herself coverings of tapestry; her clothing is silk and purple.

Her husband is known in the gates, when he sitteth among the elders of the land. She maketh fine linen, and selleth it; and delivereth girdles unto the merchant. Strength and honour are her clothing; and she shall rejoice in time to come. She openeth her mouth with wisdom; and in her tongue is the law of kindness. She looketh well to the ways of her household, and eateth not the bread of idleness.

Her children arise up, and call her blessed; her husband also, and he praiseth her. Many daughters have done virtuously, but thou excellest them all. Favour is deceitful, and beauty is vain: but a woman that feareth the Lord, she shall be praised. Give her of the fruit of her hands; and let her own works praise her in the gates.

The following are a few foundational thoughts regarding the virtuous woman of Proverbs. As you read through them, compare your life to this list. Does this passage describe you? Consider areas in which you might grow or improve.

Her value is far more precious than rubies. Do you realize how valuable you are? You are worth more than the entire world (Matthew 16:26). You are so valuable that God sent His Son to Earth to die a sinner's death on a murderer's cross to ransom your soul from hell (John 3:16; Matthew 27).

She is trustworthy. She holds her husband's heart and is a source of strength and security to him. Ask yourself—are you trustworthy? A trustworthy woman controls her tongue (James 3:5–6). She can be relied upon to be discreet, to serve as her husband's confidant, and to avoid gossip. Gossip is one of the most challenging temptations women face, but we must remember that men can also be drawn into it.

Tips to Avoid Gossip

Think before you speak. Ask yourself: Should I be sharing this, or am I trying to make someone look bad—even if what I'm saying is true?

Walk away. If you feel tempted to share a "juicy" piece of news, or if someone begins to gossip, change the subject or remove yourself from the conversation.

Keep confidences. At times, we may need to discuss difficult situations or seek support from our church family. When we do, we must be careful to remain discreet and not share those confidences with others.

Determine the root of the problem—and address it. Ask yourself whether you are speaking out of hurt or reacting to a perceived injustice. If so, work to heal and restore relationships rather than deepen division. If necessary, create healthy distance and then let the matter go.

Let it go. Some things simply do not concern us. Regardless of our opinions, they are not ours to share. Learning to let go removes the temptation to repeat them.

The virtuous woman is a willing worker. She works heartily and cares for her household. She labors faithfully as a mother, a wife, a manager of her home, a businesswoman, and a child of God. As women, we are responsible for caring for our families (Titus 2:3–5) and for teaching younger women how to do the same. As Christians, we have been called out of the world and given a responsibility—a job to do.

We must remember that we are obligated to teach others God's Word. Two of my favorite verses emphasize this truth. John 4:35 states, "Say not ye, There are yet four months, and then cometh harvest? Behold, I say unto you, Lift up your eyes, and look on the fields; for they are white already to harvest." Luke 10:2 adds, "Therefore said he unto them, The harvest truly is great, but the labourers are few: pray ye therefore the Lord of the harvest, that he would send forth labourers into his harvest." Like Christ, we must recognize the need for the gospel to be taught. We cannot simply sit back and observe. We must be willing to work in God's vineyard. We are the laborers Christ needs. Someone once said that we are Christ's hands on Earth—and in many ways, that is true.

One of the saddest statements I have ever heard was spoken to me when I was seventeen. The small congregation I attended needed a Bible class teacher for the preschool class, and the former teacher told me it was my turn. She explained that she had been teaching for years and had done enough. It was time for her to sit back, relax, and take it easy. I understand the feeling of burnout that can come after years of teaching. We all need seasons of rest and opportunities to grow through study ourselves. However, we must never adopt the attitude that we have done enough for God.

Instead, we should ask ourselves what more we can do. If teaching Bible classes has become a burden, we should consider other ways we might serve. Imagine if Christ had gone to the garden and prayed, "Father, I've preached for three years, traveled, healed the sick, and cast out demons—but this is too much. I'm afraid. I've done enough. Let someone else go to the cross. Perhaps Peter would be a good choice." Of course, Christ did not respond that way. He endured to the very end and never faltered. While we may struggle or feel weary, we can always return to God. He is waiting with open arms, just as the father waited for his son in the parable of the prodigal son (Luke 15:11–32).

The virtuous woman is also knowledgeable in business and agriculture—an aspect of her character that is often overlooked. She cared for her household and possessed the wisdom to recognize a good field and the understanding to purchase it when the opportunity arose. Scripture also provides New Testament examples of women who cared for their households while engaging in productive work.

Acts 16:13–15 records the conversion of Lydia:

"And on the sabbath we went out of the city by a river side, where prayer was wont to be made; and we sat down, and spake unto the women which resorted thither. And a certain woman named Lydia, a seller of purple, of the city of Thyatira, which worshipped God, heard us: whose heart the Lord opened, that she attended unto the things which were spoken of Paul. And when she was baptized, and her household, she besought us, saying, If ye have judged me to be faithful to the Lord, come into my house, and abide there. And she constrained us."

Lydia was a businesswoman—a seller of purple—who worshipped God and responded obediently to the gospel. Her example shows that a woman can manage business affairs while remaining faithful to God and caring for her household.

Priscilla is another example of a godly working woman. She is well known for laboring alongside her husband, Aquila, and for helping teach Apollos more accurately the word of God (Acts 18:26). She is also mentioned by the Apostle Paul as a fellow worker in Christ (Romans 16:3). In Acts 18:3, we learn that Priscilla and Aquila were tentmakers by trade. Ladies, we can be working mothers and manage a household, but we must remember that our first responsibility is to the home (Titus 2:5). What a blessing it is when we do not have to work outside the home.

A virtuous woman also helps those in need. Ruth is an excellent example. As we have seen, she left her country, family, and friends to accompany her mother-in-law into a strange land (Ruth 1–2). Dorcas is another powerful example of a woman devoted to helping others. Acts 9:36–42 records her story. She was a woman of Joppa who was full of good works and charitable deeds (v. 36). When she became sick and died, the widows wept and showed the garments she had made for them (v. 39). In verse 40, Peter raised her from the dead. There are needy people all around us, and we must be willing to help where we can.

A virtuous woman knows her family is well cared for because she has done her part to provide for them. Her children and her husband recognize her worth and value.

She fears the Lord. This is the most essential attribute of all. Proverbs 31:30 declares, "Favour is deceitful, and beauty is vain: but a woman that feareth the LORD, she shall be praised." Ruth was a woman who feared the Lord (Ruth 1:12), and we must strive to be the same.

These questions are intended to encourage discussion and further study of godly character, reputation, and faithful service. As you reflect individually or as a group, consider how the qualities of the virtuous woman can shape your own actions, relationships, and spiritual growth.

- What does the Bible teach about having a good name?
- To which other well-known woman of the Bible is Ruth compared?
- What is our value to God?
- List several practical ways to avoid gossip.
- Can we ever truly do enough for God? Why or why not?
- In what areas was the virtuous woman knowledgeable?
- Name some New Testament women who cared for their households while also working.
- How should a godly woman respond to the needs of the poor?
- How does a virtuous woman know her family is well cared for?
- What is the most essential attribute of the virtuous woman?

Refining Your Thoughts

Take a moment to reflect on what you've studied. How can you apply what you've learned? What is one thing you can do today to become a better you? Whether you are studying individually or as a class, think of practical ways to apply the lessons from this chapter in your everyday life—and commit to them. Together, we can grow as Christian women and become the kind of women God wants us to be.

Chapter Four: God Rewards the Faithful

"*But seek ye first the kingdom of God, and his righteousness, and all these things shall be added unto you.*" Matthew 6:33

THE BOOK OF RUTH TEACHES us that God rewards the faithful.

Ruth 2:15–17 reads:

"And when she was risen up to glean, Boaz commanded his young men, saying, Let her glean even among the sheaves, and reproach her not: And let fall also some of the handfuls of purpose for her, and leave them, that she may glean them, and rebuke her not. So she gleaned in the field until even, and beat out that she had gleaned: and it was about an ephah of barley."

Ruth was given a safe place to glean and was blessed in abundance. As Christians, we too are blessed beyond measure. Ephesians 1:3 states, "Blessed be the God and Father of our Lord Jesus Christ, who hath blessed us with all spiritual blessings in heavenly places in Christ." Those who are in Christ possess every spiritual blessing; those outside of Christ possess none.

In His Sermon on the Mount, Christ describes in great detail the blessings His followers will receive.

Matthew 5:1–12 states:

"And seeing the multitudes, he went up into a mountain: and when he was set, his disciples came unto him: And he opened his mouth, and taught them, saying, Blessed are the poor in spirit: for theirs is the kingdom of heaven. Blessed are they that mourn: for they shall be comforted. Blessed are the meek: for they shall inherit the earth. Blessed are they which do hunger and thirst after righteousness: for they shall be filled. Blessed are the merciful: for they shall obtain mercy. Blessed are the pure in heart: for they shall see God. Blessed are the peacemakers: for they shall be called the children of God. Blessed are they which are persecuted for righteousness' sake: for theirs is the kingdom of heaven. Blessed are ye, when men shall revile you, and persecute you, and shall say all manner of evil against you falsely, for my sake. Rejoice, and be exceeding glad: for great is your reward in heaven: for so persecuted they the prophets which were before you."

It is important to note that when Scripture uses the phrase "he opened his mouth, and taught them, saying," it signals that something of great importance is about to be spoken. Careful attention must be given to what follows.

Christ begins with the statement, "Blessed are the poor in spirit: for theirs is the kingdom of heaven." Those who are poor in spirit seek God first (Matthew 6:33) and recognize their complete dependence on Him. A person who is poor in spirit is willing to take up the cross and follow Christ (Matthew 16:24–25).

"Blessed are they that mourn." This verse is often misunderstood and applied only to those who have suffered physical loss or the death of loved ones. While it is true that God will one day wipe away all tears (Revelation 21:4), this passage refers to those who mourn over sin—whether their own or the sin of others. David expressed this sorrow in Psalm 119:136: "Rivers of waters run down mine eyes, because they keep not thy law." David wept because the people lived in sin. Sin, after all, is the transgression of God's law (I John 3:4).

How many of us have spent time in prayer, unable to find the words to express the burden of our hearts? There have been moments when the pain of my own sin—or the sin of others—was so overwhelming that all I could do was weep before God.but sob while trying to pray. God knows our needs. He understands the pain of sin, and he will comfort us if we turn to him.

"Blessed are the meek: for they shall inherit the earth."

In everyday English, meekness is often understood as being submissive or easily taken advantage of. However, that is not the meaning Christ conveys in Matthew 5:5. According to Strong's Concordance, biblical meekness is not weakness, but rather the exercise of God's strength under His control—demonstrating power without undue harshness. Christ Himself is the ultimate example of meekness.

Isaiah 53:7 describes this perfectly: "He was oppressed, and he was afflicted, yet he opened not his mouth: he is brought as a lamb to the slaughter, and as a sheep before her shearers is dumb, so he openeth not his mouth."

Matthew 26:47–56 records the scene of Christ's arrest. He did not resist or fight back. John tells us that Jesus simply asked for His disciples to be released (John 18:8). When Peter attempted to defend Him with violence, Christ stopped him and healed the ear of Malchus, which Peter had severed (John 18:10; Luke 22:50–51). Christ also stated that if He asked His Father, more than twelve legions of angels would come to His aid (Matthew 26:53). Yet He chose restraint. That is meekness.

The phrase "inherit the earth" must be understood in the broader context of Scripture. Serious Bible students know that the earth will be destroyed by fire at Christ's return. II Peter 3:10 states, "But the day of the Lord will come as a thief in the night; in the which the heavens shall pass away with a great noise, and the elements shall melt with fervent heat, the earth also and the works that are therein shall be burned up."

Wayne Jackson, in his article "Matthew 5:5—Meek Inherit the Earth," explains that "God is the owner of the earth" (Psalm 24:1). Those who obey Christ become children of God (Galatians 3:27; Hebrews 5:9) and joint heirs with Christ (Romans 8:17). God supplies all our needs (Philippians 4:19), and therefore Christians enjoy the blessings of this world more fully than others. Most importantly, our inheritance is spiritual (Acts 20:32). We are heirs in the kingdom of Christ (Ephesians 5:5), citizens of that kingdom even now (John 3:3–5; Colossians 1:13), and we look forward to an inheritance reserved for us in heaven (I Peter 1:4), knowing that the earth itself will one day pass away (II Peter 3:10).

Perhaps my favorite of the Beatitudes is found in Matthew 5:6: "Blessed are they which do hunger and thirst after righteousness: for they shall be filled." This hunger is not physical, like the hunger Ruth sought to relieve when she gleaned in Boaz's fields, but a spiritual hunger.

Several years ago, I went on a mission trip to Costa Rica. It was a blessing to teach people who genuinely wanted to learn God's Word, and it was humbling to see how people with very little were willing to share everything they had. Yet there was one thing I discovered during that trip—thirst.

Not long after arriving in Tres Ríos, I realized how badly I wanted a glass of iced tea. At that time, I still drank sweet tea, and nothing satisfied that craving. I drank water, coffee, frutas, and sodas, but nothing filled the desire. I don't know whether it was the sugar, the caffeine, the tannin, or all three combined, but for an entire week I longed for iced tea. It was always in the back of my mind, and I'm sure my husband and friends grew tired of hearing about it.

When we finally boarded our flight home, there was still no iced tea. I counted the hours until we landed in Atlanta. Once there, I ordered a sweet tea from Wendy's and drank it quickly—every last drop. I had no idea how intense that need had been until it was satisfied.

That persistent craving is what I think of when I read Matthew 5:6. It is a deep, driving desire—a hunger you will go to great lengths to satisfy. That is how we should yearn for God's Word and His righteousness.

"Blessed are the merciful: for they shall obtain mercy." We are called to show mercy to others. God has already shown us immeasurable mercy by sending His Son to die for us (John 3:16). He has promised the faithful Christian that our sins will no longer be held against us (Hebrews 8:12). We must forgive others if we expect to be forgiven (Matthew 6:14–15). Of course, this is often easier said than done.

I recently read a post in one of my Facebook groups that captured this truth beautifully. A sister asked for prayers for the man who accidentally ran over her grandmother. The grandmother had gone to check her mailbox and then turned into the road. Though gravely injured, she told the EMTs it was her fault, not the driver's. The young man was devastated and struggling deeply after the accident.

Rather than responding with anger or threats, the family showed mercy. They wanted no harm to come to him and instead asked for prayers when they learned he was considering taking his own life. Their response reflected true mercy—the kind Christ describes.

How often do we hold on to things we should release? I would hate to stand before God on the day of judgment while harboring a grudge against someone. I would hate for the one thing that kept God from showing mercy to me to be my refusal to show mercy to others.

Perhaps we struggle to be merciful because we expect more from others than we expect from ourselves. We know what people should do—often, we know exactly what we should do—but we place others on pedestals and become disappointed when they fail to meet our expectations.

My husband works for one of the largest Fortune 500 companies in the world. I cannot count how many times I have heard people say that the company is terrible because a cashier was rude, a former store manager said something unkind, or an employee failed to help them find an item. People often blame the corporation rather than the individual.

One thing I have learned from working with people is this: people are people. They are not a company, an organization, or a brand. Even the most admired Christians are not always the glorious, unspotted church—though they strive to be. People are flawed, imperfect, and sometimes simply have bad days. People say and do things they later regret, even if they never express that regret. People are shaped by their environments and the families in which they were raised. People are not always good—and neither are we. If we want mercy, we must be willing to extend mercy.

"Blessed are the pure in heart: for they shall see God." One of the most troubling aspects of Calvinist doctrine, in my view, is the teaching of original sin—the idea that a person is born sinful and bears the guilt of Adam's sin from birth. This belief stems from a misunderstanding of Psalm 51:5, which states, "Behold, I was shapen in iniquity; and in sin did my mother conceive me."

I believe the Bible is the infallible Word of God. That means Scripture is true and does not contradict itself. If Psalm 51:5 taught that David was born sinful, then Scripture would contradict itself elsewhere.

Consider the following passages. Deuteronomy 24:16 states, "The fathers shall not be put to death for the children, neither shall the children be put to death for the fathers: every man shall be put to death for his own sin." Ezekiel 18:20 echoes this truth: "The soul that sinneth, it shall die. The son shall not bear the iniquity of the father, neither shall the father bear the iniquity of the son." The Apostle Paul writes in Romans 14:12, "So then every one of us shall give an account of himself to God." If Scripture consistently teaches that individuals are responsible only for their own sins, then Psalm 51:5 must be understood figuratively.

So what does that verse mean? It may refer to ceremonial uncleanness connected to an adulterous lineage (Genesis 38; Deuteronomy 23:2), as noted by Wayne Jackson. It may also reflect the reality that David was born into a sinful world, or it may refer to his personal sin with Bathsheba (II Samuel 11). Regardless, it cannot mean inherited guilt at birth.

What disturbs me most about the doctrine of original sin is not only that it contradicts Scripture, but that it conflicts with what the Bible teaches about purity of heart and the innocence of children. A few months ago, I sat in a history class taught by a woman who identified as a Calvinist—though I do not believe she realized it. I hung my head when I heard her tell children that we know children are evil from birth because they will not share their toys.

Really? Really?

The Bible teaches that a follower of God must become like a child. Notice Matthew 18:1–6:

"At the same time came the disciples unto Jesus, saying, Who is the greatest in the kingdom of heaven? And Jesus called a little child unto him, and set him in the midst of them, and said, Verily I say unto you, Except ye be converted, and become as little children, ye shall not enter into the kingdom of heaven. Whosoever therefore shall humble himself as this little child, the same is greatest in the kingdom of heaven. And whoso shall receive one such little child in my name receiveth me. But whoso shall offend one of these little ones which believe in me, it were better for him that a millstone were hanged about his neck, and that he were drowned in the depth of the sea."

Christ clearly recognized the innocence and humility of children. He emphasizes this again in Matthew 19:14 when He says, "Suffer little children, and forbid them not, to come unto me: for of such is the kingdom of heaven."

The Apostle Paul also speaks of childlike goodness in I Corinthians 14:20: "Brethren, be not children in understanding: howbeit in malice be ye children, but in understanding be men." Think about how young children handle conflict. They may argue or become upset, but within minutes they have moved on and are friends again.

A person who is pure in heart reflects this same childlike spirit. Not only are they kind and sincere, but they genuinely seek God. Sisters, we must strive to be pure in heart. We must humble ourselves and be willing to follow God's Word.

"Blessed are the peacemakers: for they shall be called the children of God." We are commanded to live peaceably with others whenever possible (Romans 12:18; Hebrews 12:14). This can be challenging—especially for a Texas girl raised to stand her ground—but it is possible when we place our lives fully in God's hands.

Often, being peaceable means knowing when to hold our tongue. We do not always have to be right—something I still work on myself. In matters that truly do not matter, we can choose to concede. I try to teach this lesson to my teenagers. If one insists she put the cake in the oven at 5:00 p.m. and another says it was 5:05 p.m., there is no need for a full-blown argument over five minutes.

We do not always need the last word or the opportunity to reopen a wound. How many of us have been in an argument that is finally calming down, only to throw out phrases like

"Whatever," "Fine," "Do what you want," or "It's your life"? Sometimes we revisit old conflicts by saying, "Remember the time you..." or "That's not what you said last year." We all fall into this trap at times, but this behavior does not reflect the heart of a peacemaker. Sometimes, the most godly response is to swallow our words.

That said, being a peacemaker does not mean remaining silent when God's truth is at stake. Recall Christ's zeal in the temple, recorded in John 2:12–16. Christ overturned tables and drove out those who were defiling His Father's house. He was not acting peaceably, but He was acting righteously and in obedience to the will of God.

At times, people may accuse us of being unpeaceable simply because we speak the truth (Acts 4:19; 5:29). Yet we are still commanded to speak it. In II Timothy 4:2–4, Paul warns Timothy that people will turn away from the truth, but God's servants must proclaim it regardless.

Speaking the truth often brings persecution. Christ teaches that those who are persecuted for righteousness' sake will inherit the kingdom of heaven. He tells us to rejoice when others revile us or speak evil against us for His name's sake.

Persecution hurts. It cuts deeply. Some of us have experienced the pain of doing what is right while surrounded by those who choose to do wrong. It is not pleasant, but it is sometimes necessary. Most of us will never face persecution like the first-century Christians or the prophets described in Hebrews 11:32–40. Still, if we are mocked—or even lose our lives—for Christ's sake, we are promised a home with Him (Revelation 2:10).

These questions are intended to encourage discussion and further study of the Beatitudes and the spiritual blessings found in Christ. As you reflect individually or in a group, consider how humility, mercy, purity of heart, and faithfulness—even in persecution—shape our walk as Christian women and strengthen our hope in God's promises.

- If all spiritual blessings are found in Christ, how many spiritual blessings are found outside of Christ?
- What does it mean to be "blessed are those who mourn"?
- How is the word meek defined as it is used in the Bible?
- What does it mean to "hunger and thirst after righteousness"?
- Why do we sometimes struggle to show mercy to others?
- What are practical ways you can become more merciful?
- What do Calvinists teach about original sin?
- List Bible passages that contradict the doctrine of inherited sin.
- Does being peaceable mean remaining silent about error? Why or why not?
- List biblical examples of individuals who were persecuted for Christ's sake or for doing God's will.

Refining Your Thoughts

Take a moment to reflect on what you've studied. How can you apply what you've learned? What is one thing you can do today to become a better you? Whether you are studying individually or as a class, think of practical ways to apply the lessons from this chapter in your everyday life—and commit to them. Together, we can grow as Christian women and become the kind of women God wants us to be..

Chapter Five: They Followed the Law

"*If ye love me, keep my commandments.*" John 14:15

RUTH CHAPTERS THREE and four present a beautiful picture of a man and a woman who faithfully followed God's law. In Ruth 3:1–5, Naomi instructs Ruth to go to Boaz and remind him that he is one of her near kinsmen. As a near kinsman, Boaz had the right—and responsibility—to redeem the family land and raise up children in the name of Ruth's deceased husband (Ruth 3:9).

Ruth listened to her mother-in-law and approached Boaz on the threshing floor late in the evening.

Notice Ruth 3:2–8:

"And now is not Boaz of our kindred, with whose maidens thou wast? Behold, he winnoweth barley to night in the threshingfloor. Wash thyself therefore, and anoint thee, and put thy raiment upon thee, and get thee down to the floor: but make not thyself known unto the man, until he shall have done eating and drinking. And it shall be, when he lieth down, that thou shalt mark the place where he shall lie, and thou shalt go in, and uncover his feet, and lay thee down; and he will tell thee what thou shalt do. And she said unto her, All that thou sayest unto me I will do. And she went

down unto the floor, and did according to all that her mother in law bade her. And when Boaz had eaten and drunk, and his heart was merry, he went to lie down at the end of the heap of corn: and she came softly, and uncovered his feet, and laid her down. And it came to pass at midnight, that the man was afraid, and turned himself: and, behold, a woman lay at his feet."

Ruth's presence startled Boaz, but he was not displeased to see her. Scripture continues:

"And he said, Who art thou? And she answered, I am Ruth thine handmaid: spread therefore thy skirt over thine handmaid; for thou art a near kinsman. And he said, Blessed be thou of the LORD, my daughter: for thou hast shewed more kindness in the latter end than at the beginning, inasmuch as thou followedst not young men, whether poor or rich."

(Ruth 3:9–10)

Although the book of Ruth does not specify the ages of Ruth and Boaz, the text suggests that Ruth was significantly younger than her kinsman-redeemer. She valued the inward man rather than outward appearance. She did not seek a young man, nor did she seek wealth. Instead, she sought a godly man—and she found one in Boaz.

It is comforting to know that God sees our hearts and knows us for who we truly are. As the Lord told Samuel, "Look not on his countenance, or on the height of his stature; because I have refused him: for the LORD seeth not as man seeth; for man looketh on the outward appearance, but the LORD looketh on the heart" (I Samuel 16:7).

Boaz did not hesitate to fulfill his duty as a redeemer. He did not wait for a more convenient time. The very next day, he went to the city gate and approached the kinsman who was nearer than himself, offering him the opportunity to fulfill the responsibility outlined in Deuteronomy 25:5–10. At first, the man agreed to redeem the land belonging to Elimelech's family (Ruth 4:4). However, when he learned that redemption also required raising children with Ruth, he withdrew and relinquished his right to Boaz (Ruth 4:6).

Boaz then agreed to redeem both the land and Ruth. As a public sign of confirmation, the nearer kinsman removed his shoe and gave it to Boaz, sealing the transaction (Ruth 4:7–8).

Today, Christians are no longer under the Law of Moses. Paul explains this truth in Colossians 2:14: "Blotting out the handwriting of ordinances that was against us, which was contrary to us, and took it out of the way, nailing it to his cross." We now live under a better covenant—the New Testament—made possible through the death of Christ (Hebrews 9:11–18). Just as Ruth and Boaz faithfully followed the law given to them, we must faithfully follow Christ.

Ruth and her mother had known difficult times. They had endured the loss of their husbands and faced seasons of deep adversity. They experienced hunger and understood the value of hard work. As children of God, we must understand Christ's suffering, remain strong during adversity, hunger for the Word of God, and be willing to get our hands into the soil to sow the seed of the gospel (Matthew 13).

Ruth was rewarded for her diligence. She became the wife of Boaz and the great-great-grandmother of King David. Through her—a widowed Moabite woman—God's promise to Abraham was fulfilled in future generations (Genesis 12:1–3), culminating in the birth of a Savior in a humble stable and His death on the cross for the sins of the world.

As you complete this study, take time to examine yourself. Are you living for yourself, or are you living for God? If you have placed yourself before Him, you can change. Turn back to Him. Walk the walk. Talk the talk. Remember—God can use you. Never doubt it.

These questions are intended to encourage discussion and further study of obedience, redemption, and faithful living. As you reflect individually or with others, consider how Ruth and Boaz's willingness to follow God's law and act faithfully challenges us to live obediently under Christ today.

- What do chapters three and four reveal about the character and faithfulness of Ruth and Boaz?
- When did Ruth go to Boaz, and under what circumstances?
- Describe the events surrounding Ruth's meeting with Boaz on the threshing floor.
- What qualities did Ruth recognize in Boaz?
- According to Deuteronomy 25:5–10, what were the responsibilities of a kinsman-redeemer?
- What part of a person does God look at rather than outward appearance? Provide the verse.
- Under what law were Ruth and Boaz living?
- Under what law do Christians live today?
- What must a Christian be willing to do in service to God?
- Are you doing all that you can for God? Explain.

Refining Your Thoughts

Take a moment to reflect on what you've studied. How can you apply what you've learned? What is one thing you can do today to become a better you? Whether you are studying individually or as a class, think of practical ways to apply the lessons from this chapter in your everyday life—and commit to them. Together, we can grow as Christian women and become the kind of women God wants us to be.

Christian
Lost in sin, black as night,
Nowhere to turn, no relief in sight.
Filled with despair, unable to see,
But He shed His red blood to set me free.
Washed in blue water, my sins are no more,
My soul white as snow—sinless, restored.
Walking anew with my head held erect,
Seeing the green of the world with newfound respect.
The grace of His Son purchased a sinner like me,
Delivering me from evil for all eternity.
I walk by faith and hope for the mansions above,
Where I'll wear purple and gold, and the light is His love.
© Susan Elliott

References

Amazing Bible Timeline. What Jobs Did the Twelve Apostles Have and Where
Did They Hail From?

   http://amazingbibletimeline.com/bible_questions/
   q28_twelve_apostles_background/

Bible Hub. Strong's Concordance: Definition of Meekness.
http://biblehub.com/greek/4239.htm
Burton, H. Judd. Chemosh: Lord of the Moabites.

   http://ancienthistory.about.com/od/
   cgodsandgoddesses/a/chemosh.htm

Cauley, Kevin. The Beatitudes. Church of Christ Articles.

   http://churchofchristarticles.com/blog/
   administrator/the-beatitudes/

Eskew, Victor. The Book of Ruth: Introduction.

   http://www.oceansidechurchofchrist.net/Ruth/
   2012-11-13A_1___Introduction_to_Ruth.html

Jackson, Wayne. Matthew 5:5 — Meek Inherit the Earth.
Christian Courier.

   https://www.christiancourier.com/articles/905-
   matthew-5-5-meek-inherit-the-earth

Jackson, Wayne. Original Sin and a Misapplied Passage. Christian Courier.

https://www.christiancourier.com/articles/276-original-sin-and-a-misapplied-passage

Jerusalem Insider's Guide. Weather in Jerusalem. http://www.jerusalem-insiders-guide.com/weather-in-jerusalem.html
Scene of the Crime: Revisiting the Yogurt Shop Murders. Austin Chronicle.

http://www.austinchronicle.com/news/2011-12-16/scene-of-the-crime/

Shooting Rampage at Killeen Luby's Left 24 Dead. Houston Chronicle.

http://www.chron.com/life/article/Shooting-rampage-at-Killeen-Luby-s-left-24-dead-2037092.php